Gardeners'
World magazine

101 Plants for
Problem Places

10 9 8 7 6 5 4 3 2 1

Published in 2008 by BBC Books,
an imprint of Ebury Publishing
A Random House Group Company

The Random House Group Limited Reg. No. 954009

Addresses for companies within the Random House Group can be
found at www.randomhouse.co.uk

A CIP catalogue record for this book is available from the British Library.

The Random House Group Limited supports The Forest Stewardship
Council (FSC), the leading international forest certification organization.
All our titles that are printed on Greenpeace approved FSC certified
paper carry the FSC logo. Our paper procurement policy can be found
at www.rbooks.co.uk/environment

To buy books by your favourite authors and register for offers visit
www.rbooks.co.uk

Printed and bound by Firmengruppe APPL, aprinta druck,
Wemding, Germany
Colour origination by GRB Editrice Ltd., London

Commissioning Editor: Lorna Russell
Project Editor: Laura Higginson
Designer: Kathryn Gammon
Production: Bridget Fish
ISBN: 9781846074493

**Gardeners'
World** magazine

101 Plants for Problem Places
EASY-CARE IDEAS FOR DIFFICULT SITES

Author
Martyn Cox

Picture researcher
Janet Johnson

BBC
BOOKS

Contents

Introduction

Have you ever bought a plant on impulse, only to find it won't grow in your space? Don't worry, you're not alone. Many of us have snapped up a plant from the garden centre or nursery, but on getting it home have discovered it won't thrive in our soil, climate or the specific microclimate in our garden.

To ensure plants flourish, rather than limp along before finally spluttering to a halt, it pays to choose the right plant, for the right place. So how do you select perennials that will flower their socks off in a sunny border, a climber that will romp away up an exposed wall, or a ground-cover plant that will brighten up a dry patch under a hedge?

Easy. We've divided this book into six of the most problematic garden situations, and chosen the best plants that will grow in each of them – a total of 101 fabulous plants for you to choose from.

So, armed with this book, you no longer need to be disheartened about the tricky sites in your garden. Whether you have heavy clay soil or a damp and shady bed, be positive – there are plenty of inspirational plants you can grow.

Martyn Cox
Gardeners' World Magazine

Gardening terms made easy/jargon-buster

Gardening is a pretty easy hobby, but sometimes there are complicated terms for things that, once explained, are pretty straightforward. So, because we don't want anything getting between you and your gardening, we've come up with a handy glossary to help you make sense of some of the trickier gardening terms. And if you can't find the word or phrase you're looking for visit www.gardenersworld.com and check out our online glossary.

Annual – a plant that completes its life cycle (germinating, growing, flowering, setting seed and dying) within a single growing season.

Basal cutting – a cutting taken from fresh growth at the base of a plant (at ground level).

Deadhead – practice of removing dead flowerheads.

Divide or division – the means by which herbaceous stock is increased. For large plants, two forks are inserted back to back into the clump of roots and carefully prized apart to divide the rootstock. Smaller plants may be divided by hand or with a knife.

Germination – following fertilisation, germination is the sprouting of a seed into a seedling.

Half hardy – a plant that will tolerate cooler temperatures. Half-hardy plants may be grown outdoors in summer, but won't survive frosts. Half-hardy shrubs and herbaceous plants may survive an average winter in sheltered or warm environments.

Hardwood cutting – a cutting taken from dormant wood.

Hardy – plants able to withstand temperatures below 7°C (45°F).

Humus – decomposed organic matter that provides nutrients for plants and increases the soil's ability to retain water. Humus can be mixed with garden soil and sand to make a potting mixture.

Leaf mould – rotted-down leaves that are used as a mulch or soil conditioner.

Loam – rich, fertile soil, with a balance of sand, clay and humus.

Mulch – a protective top covering used to conserve moisture and suppress weeds. Materials include leaf mould, shredded bark, manure, garden compost, pebbles and black plastic sheeting.

Organic matter – rotted-down plant material (i.e. home-made compost) that is rich in nutrients and great for improving soil.

Perennial – usually refers to non-woody plants that live for more than two years or three seasons. Flowering annually, perennial plants tend to die down during winter, but have roots that will survive low temperatures.

Pricking out – the transplanting of seedlings from the seedbeds in which they were sown, to new containers.

Propagation – the processes of increasing the number of plants, including grafting, division, cuttings, seeding, budding and air layering.

Rhizome – a creeping stem that grows along or just beneath the soil surface, with roots arising from it.

Root cutting – a way of propagating plants which produce shoots, or suckers, from their roots.

Runner – an offshoot of the parent plant that runs along the soil surface, and produces roots along its length.

Semi-ripe cutting – a cutting that is taken when stems are firm and buds have developed.

Softwood cutting – a cutting taken from fresh, lush growth usually in spring.

Tender – plants that are unable to stand frost or freezing temperatures.

Japanese maple
Acer palmatum var. *dissectum* 'Seiryū'

Spectacular autumn colour

Time to plant: all year round

In autumn the normal bright green leaves of this Japanese maple undergo a dramatic transformation, changing to orange-yellow with splashes of red. The effect is sensational, and lasts for several weeks before the foliage falls to form a colourful carpet on the ground around the plant.

Although its autumnal extravaganza is memorable, 'Seiryū' is no slouch earlier in the year. From spring, its upright branches are clothed in graceful, finely cut leaves held on showy red stalks.

Slow growing, it will eventually make a 4m (13ft)-tall shrub and is perfect for planting in the dappled shade created by a larger tree. It needs moist soil and a sheltered spot to prevent the wind from scorching the tips of the leaves.

TIPS

In very cold gardens, spread a thick layer of mulch around the plant to protect it over winter. Water it well during its first spring and summer so it develops a deep root system.

False goat's beard
Astilbe

Sprays of feathery summer flowers followed by long-lasting seedheads

Time to plant: spring

A sea of feathery astilbes makes a colourful spectacle for the light shade and moist soil of a bog garden or damp border.

A large tribe of perennials native to parts of North America and Asia, astilbes mainly flower from early summer to late autumn when the showy plumes rise above clumps of deeply divided, ferny foliage. There is great diversity in this group. Some flower at ankle height, while others send up plumes 2m (6½ft) high. The colour range is limited to pink, red, white and purple, but there are many subtle variations in shade. Good varieties to try include hot pink *Astilbe* x *crispa* 'Perkeo', dark red 'Fanal' and white 'Brautschleier' (or Bridal Veil).

Resist the temptation to cut off the flower stems when they start to fade, as they soon transform into attractive brown seedheads that last well into winter.

TIPS
Remove the previous year's flower plumes in late winter. To increase your collection of plants, divide in early spring.

Brunnera macrophylla 'Jack Frost'

Icy silver leaves and sprays of tiny blue flowers

Time to plant: spring or autumn

Take a close look at its leaves and you'll see why this perennial is called 'Jack Frost' – the dark green leaves are washed with a silvery sheen, almost as if they've been touched by one of the mischievous sprite's icy fingers.

Planted in full shade, 'Jack Frost' will make a sizeable clump of heart-shaped leaves and needs well-drained, moisture-retentive soil to thrive. Don't plant it in dry soil or in a gap that dries out in summer, as the leaves will soon brown and wither.

Although it's worth growing for its leaves alone, 'Jack Frost' has another surprise up its sleeve. From April to May it produces masses of clear blue, forget-me-not flowers on delicate stems up to 55cm (22in) tall.

TIPS

Improve the soil by digging in organic material prior to planting, and add some mulch in autumn. You can propagate by dividing the clump in autumn or taking root cuttings in winter.

Camellia
Camellia x williamsii 'Garden Glory'

Masses of double pink flowers in early spring

Time to plant: all year round

Like most camellias, 'Garden Glory' needs a bit of cosseting to get the best out of it, but if you can provide its ideal growing conditions you'll be rewarded with a lavish display of drop-dead gorgeous, double pink flowers from early to mid-spring.

This evergreen shrub likes moisture-retentive but free-draining, acidic soil and needs a sheltered spot to prevent its embryonic flowers from being literally nipped in the bud by frost. If you can accommodate its needs, then don't hesitate to plant it – in a shady border, as a specimen plant in a dark corner, or under taller plants in a woodland garden.

Fast growing, this camellia makes a 4m(13ft)-tall, rounded shrub and has strong, upright growth.

TIPS
Deadhead the fading blooms. Add a mulch of leaf mould or garden compost in the autumn to retain moisture. Propagate by semi-ripe cuttings in late summer to autumn.

Clematis
Clematis 'Kasmu'

Purple climber to train into a tree

Time to plant: all year round

Many clematis are ideal for planting at the base of a tree or shrub. Their stems can be trained into the branches to provide interest to a fairly mundane plant, to cover up bare patches or provide a colourful spectacle from up high. Among the best is *Clematis* 'Kasmu', a viticella type which grows to 3m (10ft)-high and boasts crinkly, violet flowers from July to the beginning of autumn. Each bloom has a lovely velvety sheen, and an explosion of long yellow stamens protruding from its centre.

When planting to train up a tree, choose the side of the tree that is consistently damp, with soil which doesn't dry out in the sun, and enrich the planting hole with garden compost. Plant the clematis (with the cane still attached) at a 45-degree angle, so the growth can be directed into the host plant.

TIPS
In late winter, cut the top growth down to a pair of healthy buds, about 45cm (18in) above ground. Cuttings taken from mid-spring to early summer will root within weeks.

Clematis
Clematis montana var. *wilsonii*

Fast-growing climber with scented flowers

Time to plant: spring or autumn

Rocketing up to 9m (30ft) in the blink of an eye (well, it takes slightly longer than that, but it certainly grows fast), *Clematis montana* var. *wilsonii* is a lovely deciduous climber to cover a wall or fence, or train into a tree where it will clothe the branches in pretty flowers for several weeks from late spring. The four-pointed, star-shaped flowers are the purest white, with lots of long yellow stamens in the centre – don't just admire them from a distance, get up close and personal, as they smell of chocolate.

Very undemanding, it loves to grow in moisture-retentive soil and prefers to be positioned so its roots can benefit from the cool growing conditions provided by a partly shaded location.

TIPS

Add a thick layer of mulch in late winter. Plant the rootball 8cm (3½in) below soil level to avoid fungal disease. Prune after flowering to prevent the plant from getting out of bounds.

Lily-of-the-valley
Convallaria majalis

Perfumed carpet of white flowers

Time to plant: spring or autumn

You may not recognise this perennial by its botanical name, but breathe in the intoxicating scent released by its sweet spring flowers and you'll automatically know that it's lily-of-the-valley. This much-loved plant, which is native to alpine meadows, is perfect for a shady border or as ground cover under trees, spreading rapidly via underground stems to make dense clumps of broad, green leaves.

In May, the dark foliage provides a stark contrast to the tiny white bells which hang like snowflakes from the 20cm (8in)-tall, arching stems arising from among the foliage.

Ideal in dappled or full shade, lily-of-the-valley likes consistently moist soil, especially if it's improved by digging in plenty of organic material before planting.

TIPS

In autumn, divide large clumps that aren't producing many flowers and add a layer of mulch around the plants to help retain moisture. Take precautions with children as the seeds are poisonous.

Bleeding heart
Dicentra spectabilis 'Alba'

Elegant, pendulous white flowers

Time to plant: all year round

Hanging like tiny icicles, the delicate flowers of this handsome perennial make up for their diminutive size by appearing prolifically from late spring to mid-summer, helping to brighten up the gloomiest parts of the garden.

This dicentra, or bleeding heart, will thrive in a shady site under a tree or shrub, so it's great for a woodland garden or under taller-growing plants in a traditional-style cottage garden. To ensure it looks its best, plant in a fairly sheltered place as the young foliage is easy scorched by strong wind.

Growing up to 75cm (2½ft) tall, with stems which bow under the weight of the flowers, it will eventually make a large clump with showy, lime-green leaves that are deeply cut.

TIPS
To make more plants, divide in spring or when the foliage has died back in autumn. Prise large clumps apart carefully as the roots are brittle.

Bush fuchsia
Fuchsia 'Celia Smedley'

Four months of colour

Time to plant: spring

Want a plant that will flower non-stop for up to four months a year? If the answer is yes, then find a spot for 'Celia Smedley', an evergreen fuchsia whose floral display starts in July and carries on until October if the weather is mild.

The single pink and strawberry-red flowers appear prolifically and hang heavily from the branches of this vigorous shrub, which will quickly make an upright bush up to 75cm tall.

Planted with its roots in moist soil, it will grow happily in light shade and will provide you with flowers for years to come.
The catch? It's a tender perennial, so you'll need to move it to a frost-free location over winter.

TIPS
Cut back the plant by two-thirds, before lifting, potting up and storing in a frost-free place over winter. Deadhead the fading blooms to keep plants tidy. To propagate, take softwood cuttings in spring.

Bush fuchsia
Fuchsia 'Cloth of Gold'

Gleaming golden foliage and showy flowers to brighten up a gloomy spot

Time to plant: spring

Most tender fuchsias are grown for their showy flowers, which are perfect for adding a splash of quick colour in summer. 'Cloth of Gold' is no exception and has tasteful red and purple flowers that hang from the branches like dancing ballerinas, but it has an extra attribute that other fuchsias lack – shimmering golden foliage.

Ideal in moist but well-drained soil, the golden leaves which clothe the branches of this 45cm (18in)-tall bush fuchsia are perfect for adding a shaft of light in dappled shade. As they age, the gleaming lustre fades to bronze.

To protect this tender perennial over winter, cut it back by two-thirds, lift it out of the ground and place it in a small pot. Keep it just damp in a greenhouse or conservatory until spring.

TIPS

Pinch out the shoot tips when young to promote bushy growth. Encourage new flowers, and keep plants tidy by regular deadheading. Propagate by taking softwood cuttings in spring.

Coral flower
Heuchera 'Snowfire'

White-marbled leaves that turn pink in winter

Time to plant: spring or autumn

Heucheras, or coral flowers, are invaluable plants for a lightly shaded border. There have been many new varieties unveiled over the last few years, but perhaps none as good as 'Snowfire'. This eye-catching, evergreen perennial has green, scalloped-edged leaves that are heavily marbled with white. It grows to 30cm (12in)-tall and spreads to form a dense mat of foliage, topped by lots of short, slender stalks strung with dainty, red, bell-like flowers in late spring and early summer.

This heuchera will thrive in free-draining, moisture-retentive soil and is perfect for brightening up a shady patch at the front of a border. In winter it really proves its worth when the white patches turn a pretty candy pink.

TIPS
Tidy plants by trimming off any damaged leaves in early spring. Protect the crown of the plant with an autumn mulch. To make more plants, lift and divide in autumn.

Plantain lily
Hosta 'Praying Hands'

Perfect for hiding the bare legs of a tree or shrub

Time to plant: late spring or early autumn

Plug a gap under a tree or shrub with this unique hosta. 'Praying Hands' makes a perky, knee-high clump and has narrow, elongated leaves that are folded in the middle, resembling a pair of hands in prayer. The wavy edges have a narrow cream margin that stands out strongly against the dark green leaf – for the best variegation, plant it in light shade, where it will get sun in either early morning or late afternoon.

For plants to thrive, they will need moisture-retentive, well-drained soil. If necessary, add a handful of horticultural grit when planting and mulch in spring to retain moisture. When it's happy, this hosta will reward you with spikes of pretty lavender-coloured flowers in summer.

TIPS

Slugs and snails can turn leaves into paper doilies, so some control may be necessary. To rejuvenate old clumps or make more plants, lift in spring and divide with a knife.

Houttuynia cordata 'Chameleon'

Head-turning, multi-coloured leaves

Time to plant: all year round

Rather than blending into the background as its name would suggest, *Houttuynia cordata* 'Chameleon' likes to stand out from the crowd. It's a bit of a show-off, with variegated leaves splashed with green, yellow and red.

It loves wet feet, and will thrive under other plants at the edge of a pond or bog garden, or can be used as ground cover in a damp border. For the best variegation, plant this perennial in dappled rather than dense shade.

Very fast growing, 'Chameleon' spreads by underground runners and has bright red stems that contrast wonderfully with the foliage, which has a citrus scent when crushed. White flowers appear in summer, but they're not really noticeable among well-established clumps.

TIPS

Ensure you have plenty of space as this plant will grow quickly in ideal conditions, with an indefinite spread. To propagate, lift and divide plants in spring.

Hydrangea
Hydrangea macrophylla 'Veitchii'

Clouds of pure white flowers for weeks

Time to plant: all year round

The dark green leaves of this lacecap hydrangea make the perfect backdrop, allowing you to fully appreciate the glistening flowers that appear from mid- to late summer in great profusion. These graceful, flattened heads adorn the deciduous shrub for many weeks and are extremely showy, changing colour as they mature. Snowy-white flowers (which become blushed with pink and then turn red as they age) surround a cluster of smaller, lilac-coloured ones to give a fabulous two-tone effect.

Best planted in moist, free-draining soil in the dappled shade of a woodland or naturalistic-style garden, this shrub is a bit of a beast which needs plenty of space to be appreciated. It grows to 2m high by 2.5m wide (6½ x 8ft), and needs pruning annually to prevent it becoming too straggly.

TIPS

To keep plants in good shape, remove the old flowerheads in spring, pruning back to a pair of healthy buds. Also prune out any thin shoots and the occasional old branch.

Mountain hydrangea
Hydrangea serrata

A compact hydrangea for small gardens

Time to plant: all year round

While some hydrangeas are flashy showgirls, *Hydrangea serrata* is much more ladylike, with a well-behaved habit and elegant flowers. Growing to only 1.5m (5ft) high , it's a compact, deciduous shrub with pointed, oval leaves. Its size makes it ideal for a small garden, where it would look great in the middle of a border. Alternatively, try it in the damp shade of a woodland garden where it will grow happily in the cool conditions.

Sometimes known as the mountain hydrangea, this native of Japan and parts of Korea boasts flat heads of flowers at the ends of its branches, lasting from summer to autumn. The lacy flowerheads, which comprise tiny fertile flowers encircled by larger infertile ones, are pink when grown in alkaline soil and blue in acid soil.

TIPS

Keep plants compact by removing the old flowerheads in spring, cutting to a pair of healthy buds. Mulch in late winter to help retain moisture in the soil. Propagate by taking softwood cuttings in early summer.

Siberian flag
Iris sibirica

Slender spires of dramatic flowers

Time to plant: spring – summer

For a spectacular display of dark and desirable flowers, try the Siberian iris. With its feet in damp, fertile soil, this clump-forming perennial will romp away in light shade, creating a dramatic floral spectacle in late spring and early summer.

Growing up to 1.2m (4ft) high, the grassy foliage bursts from the soil in early spring, followed later by beautiful blue-purple flowers which are darkly veined and have yellow patches at the base of the lower petals. The flowers rise well above the leaves on rather slim stalks, and after the flowers die back the foliage continues to provide verdant hues until autumn.

This iris looks great in a border or next to a water feature, such as a pond or stream, and there are lots of colourful cultivars worth tracking down, including 'White Swirl' and 'Perry's Blue'.

TIPS

Cut back the dying foliage in autumn, avoiding any new leaves. Mulch with garden compost or well-rotted manure in winter. Revive congested clumps by lifting, dividing and replanting smaller pieces in late summer.

Moor grass
Molinia

Graceful sprays of late flowers and autumn colour

Time to plant: spring or autumn

Molinia is a large group of perennial grasses native to the bogs and moorlands of Europe and Asia. They are valued for their graceful sprays of flowers, which rise above clumps of slender leaves from late summer into autumn. In a breeze they sway gently, adding movement to the garden.

There is great diversity among these plants, which are perfect for adding structure and architectural shapes to a border in dappled shade. Some form knee-high clumps of only 60cm (24in), while others grow to a commanding 2.1m (7ft), and the habit can vary from an arching fountain of foliage to erect growth that looks as if it has had a few thousand volts pumped through it. In autumn the foliage of most molinias turns golden.

Good varieties to try include the butter-yellow, statuesque *Molinia caerulea* subsp. *arundinacea* 'Karl Foerster' or the more compact *Molinia caerulea* subsp. *caerulea* 'Variegata'.

TIPS
Chop tall varieties to the ground in late autumn and shorter varieties in spring. Propagate by dividing the clump in spring.

Soft shield fern
Polystichum setiferum

Architectural plant with evergreen, feathery fronds

Time to plant: all year round

Tightly clenched, small white knuckles start to unfurl in spring, reaching skywards as they open into finely divided, feathery fronds. Launched in great succession, these are elegant and downy to the touch, giving rise to its common name of soft shield fern.

Its good looks and the fact that it's an evergreen make this one of the most useful and desirable ferns you can grow. The soft shield fern provides year-round structure and colour, forming a 1.2cm (4ft) tall, upright clump that bulks out quickly to fill a space in a shady border or beneath a tree or shrub.

There are many cultivars available, some with more finely divided foliage and others that carry bulbils (small bulbs) on the fronds. They will thrive in moist but well-drained soil, in full or dappled shade.

TIPS
Improve the soil before planting by adding leaf mould. This fern can spread to 90cm (3ft) wide. Make sure you give it plenty of space so that you can enjoy its architectural shape to the full. Remove any damaged fronds in spring before new ones unfurl.

Cowslip
Primula veris

Nodding heads of sweetly fragrant flowers

Time to plant: spring or autumn

The native cowslip is a charming herbaceous perennial that looks good planted in a woodland garden, or meadow, or when naturalised in grass under the spreading boughs of a tree. Forming a rosette of textured, crinkled leaves, cowslips spread slowly to make quite dense clumps. Above these rise small flower stalks carrying clusters of nodding flowers from mid- to late spring – the butter-yellow blooms are funnel shaped and sweetly scented, attracting nectar-loving wildlife, such as bees.

To thrive and spread, cowslips need partial shade and consistently moist soil. They will also make new plants by self-seeding – if you plan to grow them in a meadow, don't cut the grass until late July so they can set seed.

TIPS
Divide large clumps to make new plants in spring or autumn. Plant young cowslips in groups for a great display. Raise plants from seed in early autumn.

Rhododendron
Rhododendron 'Dora Amateis'

White pillows of scented spring flowers

Time to plant: all year round

From mid- to late spring, a layer of white flowers covers the branches of this low-growing rhododendron, appearing in such profusion that 'Dora Amateis' resembles a pillow wearing a case woven from the finest Egyptian cotton. Despite their comfy appearance, it's probably best not to rest your head on the plant, but it's definitely one to keep close at hand – the blooms pack a spicy scent and inside each funnel-shaped flower you'll see a cluster of attractive, tiny green speckles.

Growing to only 90cm (3ft) tall, but with a spread of 1.8m (6ft), this evergreen shrub needs to be planted in well-drained, moisture-retentive, acidic soil. Try it at the front of a mixed border or in the light shade of a woodland garden.

TIPS

Add a thick layer of mulch to the soil in autumn to help retain moisture. If necessary, prune out any branches that spoil the plant's shape. Make more plants by taking semi-ripe cuttings in autumn.

Bugle
Ajuga reptans 'Black Scallop'

Carpet-forming perennial to attract butterflies and bees

Time to plant: all year round

Your garden will be buzzing with nectar-loving wildlife if you find a spot for this carpet-forming perennial. 'Black Scallop' – which is closely related to bugle, a commonly found wildflower – is an attractive ground-cover plant that spreads by overground runners to form rosettes of beetroot-purple, crinkle-cut leaves.

From late spring to the end of summer, the foliage is topped by masses of ankle-high, dark-blue flower spikes that rise gingerly from the plant and are a magnet for both bees and butterflies.

Happy in all but the driest soil, this variety is renowned for its resistance to mildew, a fungal disease which plays havoc with many other ajugas. For the best display, dig plenty of leaf mould, garden compost or well-rotted manure into the soil before planting.

TIPS

If plants become overcrowded, rejuvenate the clumps by dividing in autumn. Propagate by taking cuttings from runners in early summer.

Lady's mantle
Alchemilla mollis

Lime-green, ground-cover plant for softening the edges of beds

Time to plant: spring or autumn

Most often seen spilling over on to the edges of a sunny path from a herbaceous border, *Alchemilla mollis* is an amenable perennial that is equally at home growing under a tree or shrub, where the soil is sucked dry by thirsty roots.

It has many attributes. Plants are perfect for covering bare patches, quickly making a 50cm high by 60cm wide (20 x 24in) clump, boasting good-looking, rounded leaves with scalloped edges. In early summer, these are almost hidden by arching sprays of frothy, lime-green flowers. Deadhead these as they fade and you can enjoy a repeat performance a few months later.

Plants self-seed freely, which is great if you have lots of gaps to fill, but editing out what you don't need may be necessary to prevent them taking over.

TIPS
Before planting, improve the soil by adding garden compost or leaf mould. Cut back the foliage to a few centimetres above ground in November. To prevent self-seeding, remove the flowerheads as they fade.

Lords and ladies
Arum italicum subsp. *italicum* 'Marmoratum'

Marbled leaves and eye-catching berries

Time to plant: autumn

In late autumn, the spear-shaped leaves of this perennial unfurl slowly from the ground to reveal their gorgeous, glossy, marbled surface. Lords and ladies, as it's commonly called, is a choice plant for dappled shade and it will go on to make a large clump while growing with its feet in dry soil.

The showy leaves are long lasting and remain on the plant until the following summer when they act as a foil for a succession of 40cm (16in) tall, white flower spathes that are followed by clusters of shiny orange berries on a stout stem. This often remains long after the leaves have died back, and sometimes until the new flush of foliage appears later in the year.

TIPS
Plant new tubers 15cm (6in) deep.
You can propagate by dividing large clumps in autumn. Take precautions with children, as all parts of the plant are toxic.

Cotoneaster
Cotoneaster splendens

White flowers followed by glossy orange berries

Time to plant: all year round

With rounded green leaves that turn red in autumn, the arching branches of this deciduous shrub provide stunning late-season interest for any part of the garden in light shade. But *Cotoneaster splendens* can be relied on to provide more than just fleeting interest – in summer its branches are smothered with pretty white flowers, which are followed by jewel-like, spherical orange fruit that adorns the branches from later summer and last well into autumn (as long as the birds don't take them all).

Fairly fast growing, this cotoneaster will make a large 2m (2½ft)-tall shrub and is easy to look after. It needs very little maintenance, other than removing any damaged or dying branches.

TIPS
Before planting, improve the soil's water-holding capacity by digging in plenty of leaf mould or garden compost. Add a layer of mulch in autumn. The best way to propagate is by taking greenwood cuttings in early summer.

Barrenwort
Epimedium perralderianum

Emerald-green leaves all year round

Time to plant: spring or autumn

This epimedium is one of the most desirable perennials to grow in dry shade, making dense clumps of finely toothed, heart-shaped, evergreen leaves that will add year-round interest to the front of a shady border or a bare patch in a woodland garden.

A native of Algeria, where it grows under trees in mountainous areas, it flourishes in well-drained soil and, once established, is tolerant of drought. It's a great plant to provide colour over winter, but from mid- to late spring the foliage takes a back seat as lots of short, wiry stems emerge holding sparsely placed, pretty lemon-yellow flowers.

To help it perform well, improve the soil before planting, adding generous amounts of organic matter, such as leaf mould.

TIPS
To help lock moisture in the soil, spread a generous layer of mulch around the plants in late spring when the ground is wet. Trim off any tatty-looking leaves in spring. To make more plants, divide clumps in autumn.

Busy Lizzy
Impatiens walleriana 'Fiesta Sparkler Cherry'

More than three months of flowers

Time to plant: late spring

You either love or hate busy Lizzies – to some they're free-flowering Lilliputian gems, adored for their ability to brighten up hanging baskets, borders and containers, while others think they're old fashioned and won't give them the time of day. If you fall into the later camp, it may be time to give them another chance.

Impatiens walleriana 'Fiesta Sparkler Cherry' is a new breed of busy Lizzie with double, red and white bicolour flowers that look like miniature rosebuds and are produced in abundance from early summer until the first frosts.

Technically a perennial, this busy Lizzie is best treated as a half-hardy annual being discarded at the end of the season. It will survive in dry soil that has been improved before planting, and is happy in either dappled or quite deep shade.

TIPS
Dig plenty of moisture-retentive garden compost into the soil before planting. Consign plants to the compost bin when they stop flowering in autumn.

Mahonia
Mahonia x *media* 'Underway'

Essential scent for the winter garden

Time to plant: all year round

This evergreen shrub is as tough as old boots, with prickly, leathery leaves that demand respect and are impossible to damage. But despite being a bit of a hard nut, *Mahonia* x *media* 'Underway' keeps a secret – it's a softy at heart, especially from mid-autumn when copious upright spikes of flowers launch themselves from between the whorls of leaves at the top of each branch. The colour of newly hatched chicks, these flowers last for many weeks and pervade the still air of the winter garden with their sweet scent. As the flowers fade away, they are followed by bunches of ornamental black berries.

Unfussy about the type of soil it grows in, 'Underway' makes a neat, well-behaved plant about 3m (10ft) tall and will thrive in either full or dappled shade.

TIPS

If any leggy shoots spoil the shape of the plant, prune them right to the ground after flowering. In spring, add a mulch of garden compost around the plant. You can take semi-ripe cuttings from late summer.

Flowering currant
Ribes sanguineum 'Brocklebankii'

Golden foliage to light up shade

Time to plant: all year round

The golden foliage of *Ribes sanguineum* 'Brocklebankii' is excellent for adding a touch of glitz to a dowdy spot in dry shade. Whether it's in the shadow of a tree, wall or hedge, this ornamental currant will cheer up the garden for months, especially in spring when pendulous clusters of pink flowers sway from its branches.
These blooms contrast brilliantly with the leaves, and are followed in summer by strings of black berries.

A deciduous shrub, it will grow up to 1.2m (4ft) tall, making a compact, bushy plant that needs very little maintenance, other than removing wayward branches so it stays in shape. It's best to prepare the soil well before planting to help it retain moisture, and you should water the plant regularly until it's established.

TIPS
Improve the soil before planting by adding lots of organic matter, such as garden compost. Help to retain moisture by mulching plants in spring.
To propagate, take hardwood cuttings in winter.

Foam flower
Tiarella cordifolia

Foamy white spikes of spring flowers

Time to plant: spring or autumn

This is a choice perennial for quickly covering large patches of bare ground. Spreading by stolons (above-ground runners), it romps away rapidly in areas of dappled shade, making an impenetrable carpet of fresh, zingy green leaves. In autumn they really earn their keep by taking on an attractive tinge of brown.

The ground-covering foliage, which bears a resemblance to the lobed leaves of a maple, makes a perfect foil for the clouds of foamy flowers that appear in spring on wiry, 30cm (12in)tall stems. Each bloom is tiny, but en masse the display of pure snowy-white flowers is breathtaking.

Although this plant thrives in dry soil, it will do best if you dig in plenty of garden compost or leaf mould to help the soil stay moist.

TIPS

Spread a thick layer of moisture-retentive mulch around plants in spring. To make more plants, divide large clumps in spring.

Lesser periwinkle
Vinca minor 'Illumination'

Gleaming foliage to lighten the gloomiest corner

Time to plant: all year round

Successfully brightening a gloomy spot can be hit or miss. Some plants that thrive in dry shade have all the luminosity of a torch powered by recycled batteries which are in dire need of recharging. However, find a space for this ground-covering evergreen and it's like switching on a 150-watt light bulb.

The shoots of this lesser periwinkle are festooned with lots of small, glossy, golden leaves that turn to cream as they mature – the light centre stands out like a beacon, thanks to its dark green edge.

'Illumination' will swiftly form a dense carpet of foliage and spreads via long, trailing shoots that root into the ground. From mid-spring there's an additional treat as the plant is covered with long-lasting, star-like blue flowers.

TIPS
Although this plant thrives in dry soil, after planting you should water regularly until it's well established. To keep it within bounds, cut it back in spring.

Michaelmas daisy
Aster 'Little Carlow'

Mounds of colour to light up the autumn garden

Time to plant: spring

For much of the year, this Michaelmas daisy remains hidden in a border, its green foliage lost behind by a rainbow of colour provided by summer-flowering perennials. But in early autumn it's the turn of 'Little Carlow' to shine. From September to the end of October, this clump-forming perennial is transformed into a glowing mound of lavender blue, made up of countless small daisy flowers with a yellow, central disc.

Easy to look after, 'Little Carlow' is a tough plant that grows to 90cm (3ft) tall and will eventually spread to 45cm (18in), its mass of stems clad with long, pointed leaves. Perfect in full sun in a wildlife garden or at the back of a border with other late-flowering perennials, it will thrive in fertile soil that remains fairly moist.

TIPS

Dig plenty of leaf mould or garden compost into the soil before planting. Cut back fading stems in late autumn and apply a mulch. Divide in spring to make more plants or to rejuvenate congested clumps.

Masterwort
Astrantia major var. *rosea*

Masses of delicate pink, papery flowers held on slender stalks

Time to plant: spring or autumn

A close look at the papery blooms of this perennial reveals why it's often called Hattie's pincushion – the central dome, hemmed in by a collar of darker bracts, is studded with lots of tiny, round-headed flowers held on pin-like stalks.

Also known by the less romantic name of masterwort, astrantia has long been a cottage-garden favourite, but it looks equally at home in a contemporary planting scheme or at the front of a mixed border.

Give it fertile, moist conditions in sun or, better still, dappled shade and it will make a rosette of lobed leaves that are lost under a haze of pink flowers held aloft on wiry stems up to 90cm (3ft) tall. The flowers first appear in June and will often continue until early autumn.

TIPS
Improve the soil before planting by adding copious amounts of leaf mould. Deadhead the fading flowers to extend the display. Divide large clumps in spring or autumn.

Barberry
Berberis thunbergii '**Golden Torch**'

Dazzling golden leaves

Time to plant: all year round

Berberis thunbergii 'Golden Torch' is a slow-growing deciduous shrub that will eventually reach a little over 1m (3½ft) tall and is great for lifting the gloom of a slightly shaded spot. This is thanks to its tiny, rounded, yellow leaves that are tightly dressed on stiff, upright stems. The foliage provides a warm glow from late spring until autumn, and before falling it bears pretty traces of red and pink.

Equally happy in a sunny spot, this vibrant shrub makes a lively combination when rubbing shoulders with blue- or violet-flowered plants. To ensure it romps away, improve the soil before planting, opening it up with lots of leaf mould or garden compost.

A word of warning. Be careful when handling this plant – the stems are incredibly prickly!

TIPS
Prune lightly to keep a neat shape. Rake up the fallen leaves in autumn to prevent fungal diseases. To make more plants, take semi-ripe cuttings in summer.

Mexican orange blossom
Choisya 'Aztec Pearl'

Perfumed flowers and aromatic foliage are a feast for the senses

Time to plant: all year round

If you've ever wondered how choisya got it's common name of Mexican orange blossom, wait until the large, rounded shrub is smothered in pretty white flowers and breathe in deeply. These have a fruity whiff that can be enjoyed twice – first with a heavy flush of flowers in late spring, and again at the end of summer and into autumn, when the display is lighter.

Despite such floral delights, this dense evergreen is well worth growing for its foliage. The shiny leaves are long and slender, and have a strong peppery tang when crushed.

Growing to 2.4m (8ft) tall, 'Aztec Pearl' makes a great specimen and will thrive in heavy clay if the soil has been well prepared before planting to improve drainage.

TIPS
Prune sideshoots every two or three years to maintain a balanced shape. Remove any shoot tips damaged by frost in winter. You can make more plants by taking semi-ripe cuttings in summer.

Dogwood
Cornus alba 'Elegantissima'

Variegated leaves and fiery red winter stems

Time to plant: all year round

You can't accuse *Cornus alba* 'Elegantissima' of being workshy. This deciduous shrub makes a thicket of stems clad in attractive green and white-splashed leaves. While the foliage of this dogwood woos the eye during summer, it's in winter that it comes into its own – as the leaves fall, a framework of upright, scarlet stems is revealed.

'Elegantissima' is happy in heavy, wet soil and looks great next to a pond, in a mixed border or in a spot where the stems can be backlit by the low winter sun. It can grow to 3m (10ft) tall, but you'll get a better show of stem colour by keeping it compact – cutting it back hard in early spring.

TIPS
Prune to within 8cm (3½in) of the ground before new growth starts. Mulch with garden compost or well-rotted manure after pruning. To propagate, take hardwood cuttings in autumn.

Dahlia
Dahlia variabilis 'Fireworks Mixed'

Unusual striped flowers

Time to sow seeds: February – April

With striped flowers in lots of bright shades, including red, yellow, orange and white, this dahlia's explosive name is no exaggeration. It provides a spectacular show of colour all summer long, until the plants are cut down by frost in the autumn.

A half-hardy annual, *Dahlia variabilis* 'Fireworks Mixed' has the unique claim of being the first ever mixture of striped dahlias available as seed. Quick and easy to grow, they makes dwarf, bushy plants that will reach about 40cm (16in) tall and are ideal for planting en masse, making a dramatic statement.

These dahlias loves to grow in a sunny spot and prefer to have their feet in moist soil that has been improved before planting by digging in lots of organic material, such as garden compost.

TIPS

After the seeds germinate, transfer plants to 7.5cm(3in) pots before transplanting outside after the last frosts. Deadhead the flowers regularly to keep the display going. When the plants finish flowering in autumn, add them to the compost bin.

Dahlia
Dahlia 'Twyning's Candy'

Whopping bi-coloured flowers

Time to plant tubers: late spring

If you want dazzling flowers that appear in summer and carry on until the first frosts, 'Twyning's Candy' is hard to beat. A must for the middle of a border, it makes a thick clump of ferny foliage and sends up 1.5m (5ft) tall flower stems that carry the huge single flowers. These are about 12cm (4.5in) across, and the white petals that radiate from a sunny centre are daubed with two long red stripes.

For the best flowering display, plant in a sunny site in moist soil. In mild areas, the tubers can be left in the ground over winter, with just a thick mulch as protection. However, if your soil becomes very wet or you live in a cold area, lift the tubers out of the ground in autumn and keep them in a frost-free place until spring.

TIPS

Keep plants flowering longer by regularly deadheading the spent blooms. Before planting, improve the soil by digging in plenty of leaf mould, garden compost or well-rotted manure.

Foxglove
Digitalis purpurea 'Candy Mountain'

Unique, upward-facing pink flowers

Time to sow seeds: January – May

No, there's no need to rub your eyes in disbelief, this foxglove really does have tubular flowers which are turned towards the sky rather than swinging pendulously as normal. This unusual, perky habit is totally unique to 'Candy Mountain', and the breeders seriously considered giving it the name Viagra before common sense prevailed. Honest.

Plant it in beautiful drifts for real impact or use it to fill gaps at the back of a border. This foxglove makes a rosette of leaves, before the flower stalk emerges, rising to 1.5m (5ft) tall and putting on a colourful show in summer. Apart from being a talking point, a benefit of the upturned flowers is that it's easy to see the pretty, speckled throats.

A hardy biennial that will self-seed happily, it prefers dappled shaped and moisture-retentive soil.

TIPS
Deadhead when the flowers fade for a second flush of blooms. All parts of this plant are poisonous, so take care if children use your garden.

Marsh spurge
Euphorbia palustris

Gleaming golden foliage

Time to plant: spring or autumn

In early spring this herbaceous perennial wakes from its hibernation and pushes lots of fat buds above the ground. These grow rapidly upwards to form a large clump of gold – the stems are clad in tiny, gleaming yellow leaves that brighten up the garden until autumn, when cooler temperatures see the foliage take on orange and red tints before falling to the ground.

Perfect for a border, this euphorbia reaches about 90cm (3ft) high and its acid-yellow flower clusters perch above the foliage from late spring to early summer.

Although most of this large group of plants hate wet soil, marsh spurge (as its name suggests) revels in moist but well-drained clay, as long as it's planted in a sunny spot.

TIPS
Keep plants tidy by removing fading flowerheads (wear gloves as the sap is toxic). Provide supports to prevent the clumps flopping. Lighten the soil by digging in well-rotted manure.

Fig
Ficus carica

Showy leaves and delicious fruit

Time to plant: spring or autumn

Picking juicy, succulent figs straight from the tree is one of life's pleasures, and despite originating in warmer climes, this gourmet fruit is incredibly easy to grow in British gardens.

Figs are instantly recognisable by their large, hand-shaped leaves, and there are many varieties available, all of which love a sunny spot. The fruit develops in spring and is ready for picking in early autumn. A second crop sometimes starts to grow in summer, but it is usually stopped in it's tracks by frost.

If planted straight into open ground, figs can reach a massive 5m (16½ft) tall, so it's best to keep the plant compact by restricting its roots – plant it in a 60cm (24in) square pit with a layer of compressed gravel at the base and line the sides with paving slabs.

TIPS

Clay soil naturally restricts fig roots, but if it tends to become waterlogged over winter, improve the drainage before planting. Good varieties include 'Brown Turkey', 'White Marseilles' and 'Brunswick'.

Hydrangea
Hydrangea arborescens

Gleaming drumstick flowerheads to brighten up a shady spot

Time to plant: all year round

Need to brighten up a gloomy corner of the garden? Then check out *Hydrangea arborescens*. This deciduous shrub, which is native to woodland regions of the USA, has the perfect blooms to light up a spot in dappled shade for several months.

The creamy-white drumstick flowerheads are carried on the ends of slender, orange-brown canes from mid-July to the end of autumn, contrasting perfectly with the mass of dark green pointed leaves beneath them.

Spreading by underground suckers, this hydrangea flowers on the current year's growth and can make a very large shrub, 2.5m (8ft) high, with a similar width. However, the larger the shrub, the smaller the flowerheads, so cut it back hard for more canes and bigger blooms.

TIPS

For the best display of blooms, cut back to within 10cm (4in) of the ground in spring. It loves fertile, moist soil that has been improved with leaf mould before planting.

Apple
Malus domestica

Spring blossom and juicy fruits

Time to plant: container-grown plants all year round; bare-root plants November – March

Eating an apple picked straight from the tree is one of life's greatest pleasures in late summer and autumn, but with so many varieties available, choosing what to grow can cause some serious head scratching. The best – and most delicious – solution is to do a taste test of varieties at an apple fair. Another great option is to choose a heritage variety that was raised in your region.

Depending on what you pick, trees can reach 2–4m (6½–13ft) tall and will do well on fertile clay soil. However, apples hate wet feet, so improve the drainage with grit and well-rotted compost if your clay is particularly sticky.

If you have a tiny garden, try a minarette – these compact trees makes a vertical stem that only reaches 1.2m (4ft) after 10 years.

TIPS

Apply a thick mulch around the base of the tree in spring. Prune the tree to keep an open, goblet shape. Allow some fruit to remain on the tree or on the ground in autumn to provide food for birds.

Crab apple
Malus x atrosanguinea 'Gorgeous'

Stunning, shiny red fruit in autumn

Time to plant: all year round

Sometimes it's hard for a plant to live up to its name, but 'Gorgeous' doesn't fail. It's a real beauty with a long season of interest. In late spring the slightly arching, spreading branches are covered with pink-tinged buds that open into white flowers, while the glossy green leaves add a verdant touch until they drop in autumn. But the ace in this tree's pack are the large lipstick-red crab apples that last well into autumn. These hang in clusters from the branches, and look so perfect that you could be excused for mistaking them for fake wax fruits.

Reaching an eventual height of only 3m (10ft), this is an ideal tree for a sunny patch in a small garden and is happy in a variety of soils, including heavy clay.

TIPS
Improve the soil before planting by digging in some well-rotted manure or garden compost. Prune out any wayward branches or those that spoil its shape. Spread a thick layer of mulch over the root area in spring.

Horsemint
Mentha longifolia 'Buddleia Mint Group'

Purple flowers are a magnet for wildlife

Time to plant: spring or autumn

If this mint ever appeared on TV's *Stars in their Eyes*, it would introduce itself by saying 'Tonight, Matthew, I'm going to be a buddleia'. And it would probably win, because from mid-summer into autumn its tapering spikes of purple flowers bear an uncanny likeness to its namesake.

Commonly known as horsemint, due to its musky scent, it's a vigorous perennial which reaches 82cm (32in) high and can spread quickly, via underground stems, to fill an empty space in moisture-retentive soil.

Unlike other mints this has no role in the kitchen, but it is an attractive plant for a sunny border. The flowers that rise above the distinctly toothed, silver-grey leaves are loved by wildlife and will attract butterflies, bees and hoverflies.

TIPS
Clay soil will naturally restrict the root run, but to further control the plant's spread, plunge a large, bottomless pot in the ground and plant it in the centre.
You can propagate horsemint by dividing in spring or autumn.

Daffodil
Narcissus 'February Gold'

Cheerful golden flowers to brighten up winter

Time to plant bulbs: late summer – early autumn

Perfect for naturalising in grass, a generous drift of this cheery daffodil is all that's needed to chase away the winter blues. With swept-back golden petals and a slightly darker, snout-like trumpet, 'February Gold' provides a warming glow when there's little other colour in the garden to help lift the tail end of winter.

Although this bulb often lives up to its name and flowers in February, it sometimes makes you wait until early March. When they arrive, the flowers sit on top of 30cm (12in) high stems and point sharply downwards, a quirk of the cyclamineus group of daffodils to which it belongs.

Plant 'February Gold' in sun or dappled shade – it'll be fine in heavy clay as long as the soil doesn't become waterlogged.

TIPS
Dig a planting hole that's twice the height of the bulb. If growing in grass, wait a month or so after flowering, when the leaves have died down, before you mow.

Mock orange
Philadelphus 'Belle Etoile'

Luxuriant white flowers packing a powerful perfume

Time to plant: all year round

Find a spot for this easy-going deciduous shrub and you'll soon be nosing the air like an old-fashioned Bisto Kid to catch its heavenly sweet scent. From late spring into early summer, this beautiful variety of mock orange is laden with flowers that infuse a warm breeze with fabulous perfume.

The flowers stand out strongly against a backdrop of dark green leaves, and each white, cup-shaped bloom has a glug of Chianti red in the centre, beneath a mass of butter-yellow stamens.

'Belle Etoile' likes dappled shade or a sunny position, and will do well in the heaviest of clay as long as the soil has been cultivated to improve drainage. Growing up to 1.2m (4ft) high, with a mass of arching branches, this shrub can look untidy if left to its own devices and needs pruning to keep it within bounds or to maintain an attractive shape.

TIPS
Prune when the flowers start to fade, cutting back the flowering shoots to within a few centimetres of the ground. To keep established plants vigorous, remove a quarter of the oldest branches.

Gooseberry
Ribes uva-crispa

Succulent summer fruit

Time to plant: container-grown plants all year round; bare-root plants November – March

Pluck a ripe desert gooseberry straight from the bush in summer and you'll find it will almost melt in the mouth. The taste is simply sensational and ample reason to find space for this otherwise ordinary-looking deciduous shrub.

Growing to about 1.5m (5ft) high, gooseberries make a large bush with stems armed with dangerous-looking thorns. To thrive, give them full sun and rich, moist soil. In spring they bear tiny, insignificant flowers that attract pollinating insects and develop into rounded green, red or purple fruit a few months later, in mid-July.

Gooseberries are usually classed as cooking or desert varieties (which can be eaten straight from the plant). There are many worth growing, but among the best are the purplish 'Whinham's Industry', heavy-cropping green 'Invicta' and red 'Rokula'.

TIPS
Mulch plants well in spring. Grow as a goblet-shaped shrub and prune in winter. You can make more plants by taking cuttings in autumn.

Rose
Rosa 'Graham Thomas'

Old-fashioned English rose with a heavenly scent

Time to plant: container-grown plants all year round; bare-root plants autumn – spring

These rich yellow flowers are gorgeous, but 'Graham Thomas' is not a one-trick pony. Each of the large blooms, which measure around 10cm (4in) across, is infused with a heavenly tea scent that is at its headiest on a warm summer's day. The blooms appear from July to September.

The flowers sit on top of a 1.5m (5ft)-high shrub, which has slightly arching stems clothed with glossy, dark green leaves. It has a vigorous habit, so give it plenty of space – it will thrive with its roots in fertile clay and its branches in the sun.

While some gorgeous roses are a magnet for diseases, this variety is resistant to all the main protagonists – black spot, mildew and rust. The perfect rose.

TIPS

With bare-root plants, ensure the swollen bud union at the base of the stem is 2.5cm (1in) beneath the surface of the soil when planting. Deadhead regularly. Prune lightly after the flowers fade in early autumn.

Coneflower
Rudbeckia hirta 'Moreno'

Four months of fiery colour

Time to sow seeds: February – April

Crank up the heat with the flame-coloured flowers of this rudbeckia. Also known as a coneflower or black-eyed Susan, it has huge daisy blooms that are mahogany red in the centre with burnt orange tips. And the flowers just keep on coming for months, starting in July and often going on into October, when the plant is stopped in its tracks by frost.

Great for filling the awkward gap between ground-covering plants at the front of a border and taller plants at the back, 'Moreno' grows to 30cm (12in) high and makes a compact, bushy plant. It enjoys fertile, moisture-retentive soil.

Although it's strictly a half-hardy perennial, it's not worth the effort of trying to protect it over winter as it's so easy to grow as an annual each year.

TIPS

Raise from seed indoors, then plant out between May and June. Deadhead regularly to keep plants tidy and ensure flowering continues for months. Lift and compost plants after they've been cut down by frost.

African lily
Agapanthus 'Queen Elizabeth The Queen Mother'

Architectural perennial with head-turning blue flowers

Time to plant: spring or autumn

The African lily, or lily of the Nile, is a well-known beauty, and this distinguished variety is crowned with dark blue, rounded flowerheads that rise high above a mass of leathery, strap-shaped leaves in mid-summer. Expectation is great as it sends up a series of stately 85cm (34in) high flower stems, each topped with a bulging, papery sheath that eventually bursts open to reveal its cluster of pendent flowers.

All this perennial needs to thrive is full sun and free-draining soil that has been improved with leaf mould, garden compost or well-rotted manure before planting. Mature plants are extremely drought tolerant, so they should survive on rainwater alone. In the first and second summer after planting, it's best to water young plants whenever the soil dries out to help them get established.

TIPS
In cold areas, protect the plants over winter with a thick layer of mulch. To make more plants, simply divide large clumps in spring.

Ornamental onion
Allium stipitatum

Stately bulbs with breathtaking flowers

Time to plant: autumn

Here's a quick way to turn a dull spring border into a show-stopping display. Plant a swathe of *Allium stipitatum* bulbs, and from late May to June large, rounded pink flowerheads about the size of a cricket ball will tower over everything else on robust, 1.5m (5ft) tall stems. Grown en masse, the spectacle will blow your socks off.

From the sun-baked mountain slopes of East Asia, this allium likes to be planted in well-drained, gritty soil and, when happy, will slowly spread to increase the floral show. Although the flowers are fairly short lived, they keep their architectural beauty even when they start to fade, and as long as they aren't battered by wind and rain, the skeleton seedheads can last well into winter.

TIPS

Plant the bulbs 10cm (4in) deep, incorporating horticultural grit into the soil if necessary to aid drainage.
Divide congested clumps in spring, every four or five years.

Rock rose
Cistus Iadanifer

Non-stop flowers for weeks in early summer

Time to plant: spring or autumn

Each saucer-shaped flower lasts for only one day, but this rock rose makes up for the short-lived appearance of individual blooms by producing masses of buds over several weeks, from June to July.

From rocky hillsides across parts of the Mediterranean and North Africa, this hummock-forming evergreen shrub loves to be planted in free-draining soil. It will romp away when it can bask in the rays of the sun, producing an amazing floral display.

Rock roses reach 60–90cm (24–36in) high and are ideal for borders, rock gardens and coastal gardens. The colour range is limited to white or pink, but there are many variations in shade and petal markings.

TIPS

Prune plants after flowering to maintain an attractive shape, but avoid cutting back too hard as growth will be checked. You can propagate by taking softwood cuttings in summer.

Smoke bush
Cotinus coggygria 'Velvet Cloak'

Sensational purple foliage and billowing clouds of pink flowers

Time to plant: all year round

There are few sights more arresting in the garden than a cotinus in late summer, when its rounded silhouette is lost under clouds of wispy flowers. From a distance these look like a misty haze, giving rise to its common name of smoke bush.

Although the sight of 'Velvet Cloak' in flower is memorable, it more than earns its keep in the garden for its foliage alone. This large deciduous shrub, which will reach 4.5m (15ft) tall, has lovely purple leaves that change colour before they fall in autumn, taking on a reddish hue.

To enjoy its charms, give this shrub a sunny position in soil that drains freely. When established and well rooted, it is more or less drought tolerant.

TIPS

Minimal pruning is required – simply remove any branches that spoil the shape. To propagate, take softwood cuttings in summer.

Pink
Dianthus 'Lily the Pink'

Traditional flowers with a knock-out scent

Time to plant: spring

A quintessential plant for a traditional cottage garden, pinks are back in fashion thanks to the trend for growing your own cut flowers. 'Lily the Pink' is particularly recommended for displaying indoors due to its extra-long flower stems, 40cm (16in) that hold lots of double, slightly fringed, lavender-coloured flowers with a powerful, spicy perfume.

Happy in well-drained soil in a sunny border, 'Lily the Pink' can be used to plug gaps or can be planted in a row among edible crops in an ornamental vegetable garden. This evergreen perennial makes a mat of bluish-green grassy foliage and flowers prolifically from May to June.

Avoid planting it under overhanging trees or other garden features, where rain can drip down into the foliage, causing the crown to rot.

TIPS

For the best perfume, don't cut the flower stems when the buds are too tight. Snip off the spent flowers for a second flush in autumn. You can take cuttings in July.

Coneflower
Echinacea 'Art's Pride'

Glowing orange flowers, adored by bees

Time to plant: spring or autumn

If you grow this coneflower, remember to duck when the large, sweetly scented flowers appear – bees and butterflies find them simply irresistible and will flock to this herbaceous perennial in great numbers.

The flowers open from June to September, and the swept-back, slender orange petals enclosing a dark brown cone are shown off to great effect on 90cm (3ft) tall, stiff stems. These stand well proud of the clump of heavily toothed, dark green leaves.

This is an easy-going plant that suits many styles of garden. Perfect in a border, cottage garden, wildlife garden or prairie-style planting, all 'Art's Pride' needs to provide its long-lasting, wildlife-attracting flowers is good drainage and full sun.

TIPS
Deadhead the fading flowers. Spread a 5cm (2in) layer of mulch over the soil in autumn. To propagate, simply divide the big clumps of foliage in autumn or spring.

Coneflower
Echinacea purpurea 'White Swan'

White daisies for late-summer colour

Time to plant: spring or autumn

Coneflowers are Cinderella plants – for many months the clumps of slightly hairy, dark green leaves are barely worth a second look, but then mid-summer arrives and you can't keep your eyes off them. 'White Swan' is particularly worth checking out, thanks to its CD-sized flowers which are held on stout, 60cm (24in)-high stems for months.

The daisy-like flowers are composed of a ring of slender white petals arranged around a domed orange centre. Long lasting, they appear from July into autumn and attract bees, butterflies and moths.

At home in a sunny border or a prairie-style planting, this perennial will romp away in well-drained soil, improved with leaf mould or garden compost.

TIPS

Deadhead the flowers as they fade.
To make more plants or rejuvenate large clumps, divide in spring or autumn.

Rock rose
Helianthemum 'Hartswood Ruby'

Makes a carpet of colour for months on end

Time to plant: all year round

Do you have a dry bank, a gap to plug in a sunny rock garden or a space at the front of a border? Then check out 'Hartswood Ruby', a new variety of rock rose that will form a carpet of colour from May until mid-summer.

The dark pink, saucer-shaped flowers with a yellow centre are sprinkled liberally over the grey-green foliage of this low-growing evergreen shrub, which spreads quickly via a network of wiry branches to form a dense, ground-covering carpet.

It's dead easy to grow and very undemanding. Just give it the sunniest spot in your garden – this is essential as the flowers will only open when the sun is at its most intense.

TIPS
Trim the plant lightly as the flowers fade for a second flush in late summer. To make more plants, take softwood cuttings in late spring.

Daylily
Hemerocallis 'Night Beacon'

Copious velvety flowers on stately stems throughout summer

Time to plant: spring or autumn

No one could ever accuse *Hemerocallis* 'Night Beacon' of being shy and retiring – with swept-back maroon petals and a chartreuse centre, this daylily's flowers are a great success.

The blooms are borne on elegant 70cm (28in)-tall stems that rise well above the clump of strap-shaped, evergreen leaves. Each flower lasts for only one day, but don't worry, they appear in abundant succession from June to the end of summer.

For a head-turning display, grow this herbaceous perennial in large swathes in a border or arid garden. It loves sun and good drainage, and is extremely drought tolerant. Plants do best if leaf mould or garden compost is dug into the soil before planting.

TIPS
Revive congested clumps by lifting and dividing in spring or autumn. Mulch plants in autumn.

Bearded iris
Iris 'Dusky Challenger'

Dark and desirable chocolate-scented flowers

Time to plant: late summer – early autumn

Find a gap in a border so you can enjoy these darkly decadent, slightly ruffled flowers in early summer. However, this bearded iris comes with a word of warning. If you're counting the calories, avoid growing it in your garden as one sniff of its cocoa-scented flowers may have you rushing to the shops to stock up on your favourite bars.

The flowers emerge on long, stout stems from late May to the end of June, rising 90cm (3ft) above a fan of sword-shaped leaves. Like all bearded irises, 'Dusky Challenger' prefers well-drained, neutral soil and thrives in a sunny spot. It hates to rub shoulders with other plants, so give it plenty of space to spread and this will also ensure air can circulate freely.

Now go on, indulge yourself.

TIPS
Improve clay soil before planting by adding garden compost. Cut the leaves back to 15cm (6in) in late autumn. Every three years, rejuvenate large clumps by dividing in late summer.

Bearded iris
Iris 'Olympic Challenge'

Bearded iris that flowers twice

Time to plant: late summer – early autumn

What could be better than a late spring-flowering bearded iris? Well, how about a variety that flowers again, putting on a second great display from August until the first frosts? Unlike most 'beardies' (as they're sometimes known among the cognoscenti), which flower mainly between May and the end of June, 'Olympic Challenge' has a second flush of rich orange, slightly ruffled blooms, making it doubly good value.

Growing up to 90cm (3ft) tall on beefy stems, this is a lofty perennial that should be grown in a sunny border. To thrive, it needs plenty of space, with rhizomes planted about 40cm (16in) apart. This iris grows well in clay, but you should improve the drainage before planting if the clay is very heavy.

TIPS

Before planting the rhizomes in heavy clay, improve the drainage by digging in lots of coarse sand. You can make more plants by dividing large clumps in summer. The cut flowers make excellent indoor displays.

Red-hot pokers
Kniphofia 'Dingaan' and *Kniphofia uvaria*

Stately spikes of late-summer flowers

Time to plant: spring or autumn

Red-hot pokers are a large group of architectural perennials that make dense clumps of foliage beneath spikes of fiery flowers. There is great diversity in the group, and it's possible to pick varieties to give you a continuous show of colour from late spring to the end of winter.

For a brilliant display from mid-summer to mid-autumn, try combining *Kniphofia* 'Dingaan' with *K. uvaria*. Both grow to about 1.2m (4ft) tall and are perfect in a coastal garden, tropical border or gravel garden. 'Dingaan' has stout spikes topped with bronze-green buds that open into bronze-yellow flowers, while *K. uvaria* has brilliant red blooms that fade to yellow as they mature.

Red-hot pokers love full sun and need well-drained soil to prevent the crowns rotting.

TIPS
Keep the display going for longer by removing flower spikes as they fade. Protect the crown of the plant over winter by mulching. To make more plants, divide large clumps in spring.

Red-hot poker
Kniphofia 'Tawny King'

Long-flowering red-hot poker

Time to plant: spring or autumn

If you're looking for an eye-catching perennial to add drama to your garden, then try *Kniphofia* 'Tawny King'. It produces stately flower stems that soar above the huge clumps of narrow green leaves.

Although this variety is a fairly new introduction, it's extremely popular. Why? Each 1.2m (4ft)-high bronze flower stem is topped with a scrumptious flowerhead made up of masses of apricot buds that turn cream as they open. These appear from July right through to October, making it one of the longest-flowering varieties available.

'Tawny King' looks good in a Mediterranean-style planting among rocks, in a late-summer border or even a low-maintenance urban planting scheme. It likes to bask in the sun, in free-draining or even quite poor soil. For the best results, add plenty of garden compost before planting.

TIPS
Large clumps may be shy to flower, so lift and divide plants in late spring every three years or so. In colder areas, protect plants over winter with a thick layer of mulch.

Lavender
Lavandula angustifolia 'Royal Velvet'

Great for wildlife, with highly scented leaves and flowers

Time to plant: all year round

Nothing is more evocative that sitting in your garden on a warm summer's day and enjoying the unmistakable scent of lavender being carried on the breeze. It's instantly calming, and for the strongest scent a sunny, sheltered spot is essential, allowing this English lavender to exude its essential oils.

'Royal Velvet' has tiny grey-green leaves and makes a bushy plant, about 75cm (2½ft) tall. From mid-summer, the foliage is concealed by lots of long, slender flower spikes clad in dark purple buds that open to reveal violet blooms. These soon become a magnet for bees and butterflies.

This lavender is drought tolerant and looks good planted in a swathe by the side of a path, or placed so you can enjoy its aroma from a seating area.

TIPS
Trim the spent flowerheads in early autumn to leave a well-balanced shape – avoid cutting into the old wood.
Propagate in spring by taking softwood cuttings.

Nerine
Nerine 'Lavant'

Head-turning autumn flowers

Time to plant: early spring

Fancy a change from the conventional fiery shades associated with autumn? Then check out nerines, a large group of bulbs that originate from southern Africa and make their presence known from late summer until October.

Ideal in a sunny border, rock garden or planted in well-drained soil next to a fence or wall, nerines grow to 30–60cm (12–24in) tall and spread to form a sizeable clump that makes a dramatic spectacle – masses of stout stems support a cluster of curled petals that surround lots of slender stamens.

Although some nerines are tender and need the protection of a greenhouse, many are ideal in the garden. The most common colour is pink, such as 'Lavant', but if it's white you want, look for 'Latu', or for coral-orange choose 'George'.

TIP

Plant so the nose of the bulb is just above the surface of the soil. To make more, divide clumps after flowering. Protect over winter by covering with a deep mulch of leaf mould.

Oriental poppy
Papaver orientale 'Spätzünder'

Exquisite flowers with petals like crêpe paper

Time to plant: spring

In late spring this oriental poppy sends up a multitude of egg-shaped buds, and each one splits open to reveal a crumpled cluster of petals that slowly unfurls to form a large, opulent flower.

These glossy red blooms, with their distinctive black blotch at the base of each petal, are a head-turning sight in the garden. Produced from May to July, the flowers stand on rigid, hairy stems, up to 75cm (2½ft) tall, above a dense clump of hairy, toothed leaves.

A native of rocky mountainsides in parts of western Asia, oriental poppies put on a brilliant show in a sunny, dry spot. Although 'Spätzünder' is fine planted singly, you'll make more of an impression by planting large numbers to get a sea of fluttering red flowers.

TIPS
When the display finishes, either cut back the tatty foliage and faded flower stems to promote fresh growth or simply leave it and enjoy the long-lasting pepperpot seedheads. To make more plants, lift and divide in late summer after flowering.

Oriental poppy
Papaver orientale 'Türkenlouis'

Drop-dead gorgeous flowers, the colour of lipstick

Time to plant: spring

Despite making only a fleeting appearance, oriental poppies are glamorous perennials grown for their large, ravishing flowers. 'Türkenlouis' has more va-va-voom than most. From June to July it makes its presence known with a flurry of large, cup-shaped flowers that are the colour of Marilyn Monroe's lipstick and have a deep black centre.

The heavily fringed flowers, which are the texture of paper, are carried on 80cm (32in)-tall stems that rise above thick clumps of hairy, serrated green leaves. 'Türkenlouis' thrives in a sunny position with good drainage.

After flowering, either cut back the top growth to promote a fresh flush of foliage, or enjoy the architectural seed pods that hang on for several months.

TIPS
Propagate by dividing large clumps in late summer or early autumn. If you want lots of plants, take root cuttings in early autumn.

Zonal pelargonium
Pelargonium Foxy

More than three months of colour

Time to plant: spring

Many pelargoniums are native to the mountains and deserts of South Africa, which explains their love of sunshine and their ability to withstand long periods of drought. Foxy is no different. Plant it where the sun beats down and it will often flower non-stop from late spring until autumn.

Known as a zonal pelargonium, due to the dark ring-like markings (or zones) on the rounded leaves, this frost-tender perennial grows into a bushy plant and has thick, fleshy stems that carry the clusters of semi-double, dark purple flowers over a long period.

For the best display, give plants a high-potash feed every couple of weeks and pinch off the blooms as they fade.

TIPS
Lift the plants, cut back the top growth to a third, then pot them up and overwinter in a frost-free place. You can make more plants by taking semi-ripe cuttings in mid-summer.

Ornamental millet

Pennisetum glaucum 'Purple Majesty' F1

A stately grass with velvety purple leaves and feathery seedheads

Time to sow seeds: January – March

Who could resist touching the fluffy purple seedheads that rise up from this grass on 1.2m (4ft)-high stems from mid-summer to autumn? Not many. But it has a lot more going for it than just its 'stroke me' qualities – the seedheads are a magnet for hungry birds and it's perfect for adding colour and height to a border display.

This ornamental millet is really easy going and extremely tolerant of dry conditions. For the best colour, give plants the sunniest spot possible.

Although they're technically half-hardy perennials, keeping the plants alive over winter is hard work, so they're best treated as annuals. Growing from seed is cheap and easy, but you can cheat and buy plants from early summer.

TIPS

Despite being fairly drought resistant, plants do best if well watered after planting. Deadhead the fading flower spikes. Remove plants when they finish flowering, chop them up and add to the compost.

Rosemary
Rosmarinus officinalis var. *angustissimus* 'Benenden Blue'

Aromatic foliage to fill your garden with spicy scent

Time to plant: all year round

If this plant was on a package holiday, it would forget about excursions to historical sites and spend its entire trip basking by the pool. Like all rosemary, 'Benenden Blue' is an absolute sun-worshipper and loves to catch some rays, with its roots in hot, dry soil.

Growing to 1.5m (5ft) high, this evergreen shrub has a loose, upright shape. Its branches are clothed in masses of needles, which are much finer than those on the common rosemary and exude a spicy scent. In spring and early summer, the plant is studded with lots of tiny, dark blue, tubular flowers.

Plant this rosemary in a herb garden, shrub border, as an informal hedge, or in a seaside garden where it'll thrive because it tolerates salty winds.

TIPS
This shrub can quickly become untidy, so maintain an attractive shape by lightly pruning after flowering. You can make more plants by taking softwood cuttings in spring.

Rosemary
Rosmarinus officinalis 'Sudbury Blue'

Knockout scent from a reliable evergreen shrub

Time to plant: all year round

Plant 'Sudbury Blue' close to your outdoor dining area or barbecue as the dark green needles that envelope its sturdy, erect branches are highly aromatic, especially when the sun beats down, allowing it to infuse the air with scent from its essential oils.

This evergreen shrub loves to be planted in free-draining soil in full sun, and grows to a height of 1m (3½ft). It's an upright plant that will flourish by the seaside, in a herb garden or among other shrubs and perennials in a mixed border.

From March the stems are studded with lots of tubular blue flowers that last for several weeks and are irresistible to bees and butterflies. The first flush of flowers is often followed by another in late autumn.

TIPS
Keep plants looking good by trimming lightly after flowering. Spread a mulch around the base in autumn. It's easy to propagate by taking softwood cuttings in spring.

Sage
Salvia officinalis

Spicy leaves and a magnet for bees

Time to plant: all year round

There are many perfect culinary partnerships, from fresh mint and new potatoes to tomatoes and basil, but perhaps none is more famous than sage and onion. When combined with sausage meat they make a delicious stuffing to accompany meat and poultry.

Apart from common sage's savoury tang, which can be used to perk up many dishes, it's an attractive plant for a sunny position. Growing to 60cm (24in) tall, the bushy, evergreen shrub has elliptical grey-green leaves that are rough on the upper side and slightly woolly underneath. Spikes of bluish flowers rise above the plant from early summer and are soon alive with flitting butterflies and busy bees.

Extremely drought tolerant, sage loves dry conditions and absolutely hates wet feet, especially over winter, so ensure the soil is well drained before planting.

TIPS
Prune lightly in spring to increase bushiness and again after flowering. For more plants, take cuttings in late spring. Replace plants when they become woody – every four years or so.

Irish yew
Taxus baccata 'Fastigiata'

Evergreen columns for height and winter structure

When to plant: all year round

There's nothing flashy about the Irish yew. While there are many trees with amazing foliage, showy flowers or colourful fruit, this evergreen conifer looks exactly the same in winter as it does in summer. So why grow it? Well, for its bolt-upright, columnar shape. In a large formal garden, a pair of statuesque yews makes a dramatic frame for the entrance to a 'garden room', while a single specimen is an imposing focal point. However, this plant is extremely slow growing, so a small one will fit a more compact space for many years before it will need to be evicted.

'Fastigiata' eventually reaches 10m (33ft) tall and grows well in the driest of soils. In summer its dark green leaves are a great foil for colourful perennials, while in winter it earns its keep by providing height, structure and interest. Be careful if you have young children, as most parts of the plant are poisonous.

TIPS
Prune lightly, if necessary, to maintain a tight shape. To make more plants, take cuttings in late summer. Plants can be grown as a hedge.

Verbena
Verbena bonariensis

Airy spires of purple

Time to plant: all year round

This tall, elegant perennial with long, wiry stems topped by purple tufts of flowers is one of the most versatile plants you can grow and is suitable for many styles of garden. Try it in a gravel garden, where it will thrive with very little water, or threaded between other plants in a hot border, in a prairie-style planting or a display of exotics.

So what's the catch? Well, none. All it needs is a sunny spot with well-drained soil and it will bloom its socks off, producing masses of branched 2m (6½ft)-tall flower stems from late spring until well into autumn.

Caring for it couldn't be easier. Give it a splash of water if it starts to flag and be prepared to edit out any unwanted self-seeded plants.

TIPS
Although it's hardy down to -10°C, plants still need protecting over winter – cut back to 15cm (6in) in October, then mulch the crown with a thick, insulating layer of bark chippings or garden compost.

Japanese wisteria
Wisteria floribunda 'Rosea'

Fast-growing climber with highly scented flowers

Time to plant: all year round

If you've got a large, empty space that needs covering quickly with a climber, try *Wisteria floribunda* 'Rosea'. This variety of Japanese wisteria twines itself rampantly up to a height of 9m (30ft) and is ideal for training against a sunny wall or fence, or over an arch or arbour. It is, perhaps, best suited to a garden structure you can walk through as the long racemes of creamy pale-pink flowers that drip pendulously from the stems from late spring are incredibly fragrant, and the still air of a tunnel or pergola will intensify the perfume.

As the flowers fade, the plant bears masses of furry seed pods among the lush foliage, which is produced in great abundance. Not for the lazy gardener, it needs pruning twice a year to keep it tidy and productive.

TIPS

Prune in summer and then in winter to keep plants tidy and flowering strongly. To propagate, take basal cuttings in early summer and root in a propagator.

Ornamental onion
Allium oreophilum

Fast-spreading bulb with pink flowers

Time to plant bulbs: late summer – early autumn

Native to parts of eastern Asia, this ornamental onion is found growing on rocky mountain-sides (*oreophilum* means mountain-lover in botanical Latin), where its roundish clusters of dark pink, bell-shaped flowers rise demurely on slight, ankle-high stems during late spring and early summer.

Due to its pint-sized stature, this sun-loving bulb needs to be planted where it can be seen easily, for example among stones in a rock garden or at the front of a border. It will romp away in well-drained alkaline soil, spreading quickly to make an impressive patch of spring colour. The stonier the ground, the better, as the bulbs will rot if subjected to too much winter wet.

TIPS

Plant the bulbs 12cm (4½in) deep, improving the drainage with grit if necessary. Propagate large colonies by lifting and dividing offsets in autumn, when they are dormant.

Marguerite daisy
Anthemis 'Susanna Mitchell'

Masses of summer daises to attract wildlife

Time to plant: spring

If you want to attract wildlife into your garden, consider planting this anthemis – bees and butterflies love the abundant creamy-white daises with sunny centres that cloak this hardy perennial for many weeks in summer. Perfect for the front of a border or a gravel garden, 'Susanna Mitchell' is a low-growing, mound-forming plant, reaching only 30cm (12in) high and spreading to around 60cm (24in). Although this marguerite daisy is mainly grown for its profusion of pastel flowers, it remains attractive all year round, forming a carpet of silvery, ferny foliage.

This plant does well in chalky, free-draining soil and, once established, is fairly tolerant of drought. Really easy to care for, its biggest enemy is winter wet.

TIPS
Trim lightly after flowering to retain an attractive shape. To make more plants, root softwood cuttings in spring.

Barberry
Berberis x *lologensis* 'Apricot Queen'

Hard-working shrub with gorgeous spring flowers

Time to plant: all year round

'Apricot Queen' works hard in every season. This large shrub is densely covered in small, prickly, evergreen leaves that add verdant colour 365 days a year, while in spring its arching branches are heavily laden with golden-yellow flowers. The display is at its best during April and May, but flowers often continue into summer, in lesser numbers. And if that isn't enough, it really earns its keep by producing dark purple ornamental fruits in autumn.

Eventually reaching 2m (6½ft) tall, this barberry is very easy to look after and would suit a spot in the middle of a mixed border. It's not particularly demanding about growing conditions – it's happy in sun or part shade, and will do well in a variety of soils, including chalk.

TIPS
Minimal pruning is required – if necessary trim lightly after flowering to keep within bounds. Make more plants by taking semi-ripe cuttings of this prickly plant in summer (remember to wear gloves).

Blue mist

Caryopteris x *clandonensis* 'First Choice'

Butterflies love its dark purple summer flowers

Time to plant: spring or autumn

Caryopteris thrives on alkaline soil, but with so many different varieties to choose from, which should you go for? The name 'First Choice' is a strong clue. Growing only 90cm (3ft) tall, this shrub flowers from mid-summer until autumn. Its tight clusters of blue buds open to show dark purple flowers that are popular landing pads for visiting butterflies.

'First Choice' is slightly shorter and more compact than many others caryopteris, making a well-behaved mound of greyish-green foliage – in common with the rest of its tribe, its leaves are aromatic when crushed. It is also very tolerant of drought, which ensures that the plant keeps looking good throughout a long, hot summer.

TIPS

Prune all stems back hard to healthy buds in early spring, but avoid cutting into woody stems. You can propagate it by taking softwood cuttings in late spring.

Bluebeard
Caryopteris x *clandonensis* 'Summer Sorbet'

Superb foliage from spring into autumn

Time to plant: spring or autumn

'Summer Sorbet' is a stunning new caryopteris with lively foliage that adds a colourful splash to borders for most of the year. A small deciduous shrub reaching around 90cm (3ft)-high, it carries green and chartreuse variegated leaves that provide a vibrant backdrop to its clusters of deep blue flowers. The blooms crown the plant from late summer and last well into autumn, enticing squadrons of bees, butterflies and other beneficial insects.

Like all caryopteris, 'Summer Sorbet' detests damp conditions, but give it well-drained, chalky soil in a bright, sunny spot and it should flourish. Once it's established, it's a fairly low-maintenance shrub that only needs an annual prune to keep it in shape. In time it will become drought tolerant, needing very little water to thrive.

TIPS
Cut this shrub back hard in spring, pruning to a healthy pair of buds near ground level. Aim to create a framework, but avoid cutting into woody stems.

California lilac
Ceanothus 'Blue Cushion'

Neat mounds of blue flowers

Time to plant: all year round

Evergreen shrubs are worth their weight in gold, providing year-round colour and structure in the garden. But if they also flower like billy-o for weeks at a time, they become even more precious and it's hard to put a price on them. *Ceanothus* 'Blue Cushion' is such a plant. This mound-forming variety of California lilac makes a 1.5m (5ft)-high pillow of growth, spreading to 2.4m (8ft), with its arching branches clothed in finely serrated, dark green leaves. From late winter to spring the canvas of dark foliage is transformed when the branches are peppered with tight little buttons of dark blue.

'**Blue Cushion'** will flourish in full sun and is happy in all but the shallowest of chalky soils.

TIPS
Trim lightly after flowering to maintain an attractive shape, and apply a thick mulch over the soil following pruning. To propagate, take semi-ripe cuttings in mid-summer.

Spurge
Euphorbia 'Blackbird'

Lime-coloured flowers combine dramatically with near-black leaves

Time to plant: spring or autumn

In dappled shade the leaves of this spurge are purple, but plant it in well-drained soil in full sun and the foliage deepens several shades, turning almost jet black. This dramatic quality helps 'Blackbird' provide interest in the garden all year round, but there's no doubt it's at its best in spring. From March to May the plant is topped by lots of frothy, acid-green flowers that make a striking contrast to the leaves.

A relation of the popular variety 'Redwing', 'Blackbird' is a handsome newcomer which makes a compact mound, around 45cm (18in) high. This perennial looks good in a border, rock garden or gravel garden, where it will become tolerant of drought once established.

TIPS
Take care when handling as the leaves and stems exude a toxic white sap. Prune back any tatty-looking stems in early spring. You can propagate it by taking basal cuttings in early summer.

Summer hyacinth
Galtonia viridiflora

Cool green flowers in late summer

Time to plant: early spring

This bulb is a star of late summer, when a series of robust, arching flower stems rise high above the clumps of imposing, strap-shaped grey leaves. Each stem holds more than 20 waxy, pale green flowers that open in succession, starting from the bottom and working their way to the top of the flower stalk.

From South Africa, where it grows in moist ground, this galtonia will flourish in full sun, growing up to 1m (3½ft) tall and flowering from August to September. Plant the bulbs in well-drained, moisture-retentive, alkaline soil that doesn't dry out when the plant is in growth.

Give it a thick layer of mulch in autumn, but in cold climates or areas that get a lot of rainfall, lift the bulbs, pot them up and keep in a frost-free place until spring.

TIPS
Plant the bulbs 10cm (4in) deep. Cut back the foliage when it has started to die back. Propagate by removing any rooted offsets in spring.

Lupin
Lupinus 'The Chatelaine'

A striking partnership for early summer

Time to plant: spring

Rising above clumps of green, hand-like foliage in early summer, the flower spikes of *Lupinus* 'The Chatelaine' are caught in sharp relief when grown against the blue backdrop of *Ceanothus* 'Cynthia Postan', a large mound-forming shrub.

The lupin's showy pink and white bicolour flowers open from the bottom of each 90cm (3ft) spire and work their way to the top, providing vertical colour in a traditional cottage garden, mixed border or seaside planting scheme until the middle of summer.

Both the lupin and ceanothus are really easy to grow, enjoying a sunny location and free-draining, chalky soil. Although the flowering combination is short lived, lasting just a few weeks, the ceanothus will continue to provide evergreen structure all year round.

TIPS
Remove the lupin's fading flower spikes to encourage a later, second flush.
To propagate the lupin, take basal cuttings in mid-spring.

Field poppy
Papaver rhoeas 'Mother of Pearl Group'

Subtle flowers for quick colour

Time to sow: spring or autumn

Watching the flowers of this beautiful mixture of annual poppies open is reminiscent of a butterfly emerging from its chrysalis. In summer the bristly buds of 'Mother of Pearl Group' split open to reveal a ball of crumpled petals that slowly unfolds in the heat of the sun like the wings of an emerging butterfly.

The flowers are ravishing – from subtle shades of greys, soft pinks and dusty blues to those speckled with red, white and cream. Others have petals thinly edged with white or cream.

Sow the seed in sun or part shade on well-drained, limy soil – either in spring or autumn if you live in a mild area and want earlier flowers. Allow the plants to self-seed for a repeat performance next year.

TIPS

Before sowing, prepare the soil well. Remove any weeds, fork over and rake level to leave a fine finish. Scatter the seeds, rake in gently and water. Thin the seedlings to 30cm (12in) apart.

Opium poppy
Papaver somniferum var. *paeoniiflorum*

Lavish pink flowers followed by architectural seed pods

Time to sow: March – May

Its name may be a bit of a mouthful, but fortunately this sumptuous opium poppy is a lot easier on the eye than it is to pronounce. A hardy annual, it thrives in free-draining, stony ground, making a clump of serrated, glaucous blue, topped in summer by stately flower stalks up to 1.2m (4ft) tall.

The moment this poppy comes into flower is memorable – each bud bursts open to reveal a tight mass of crumpled petals, like a scrunched-up ball of tissue paper, before unfurling into a large, fully double flower which measures about 10cm (4in) across.

After the flowers start to fade, this poppy continues to add interest thanks to its long-lasting, plump seed pods that can be left standing in the border or picked and dried for indoor displays.

TIPS

Choose a sunny site and prepare the soil before sowing, removing weeds, turning it over with a fork and raking to a fine finish. Broadcast the seeds or sow them in rows.

Coneflower
Rudbeckia laciniata 'Herbstsonne'

Imposing summer perennial with masses of yellow daisies

Time to plant: spring or autumn

A lofty perennial for the back of the border, *Rudbeckia laciniata* 'Herbstsonne' is an unforgettable sight from the middle of summer, when its robust branching stems reach high into the air and the tiny buds at the end unfurl into large, sunny daisies. Each bloom is about 12cm (4.½ft) wide and the swept-back petals are arranged around a chartreuse cone.

At about 2m (6½ft) high, this stunning coneflower draws admiring glances and the glowing, golden flowers, which tower above a thick clump of heavily veined, oval leaves, continue well into autumn.

For the best show, give it sun and well-drained soil that doesn't dry out. Shallow, chalky soil should be improved with plenty of organic matter before planting.

TIPS

Cut plants to the ground in early winter, then protect them with a generous layer of mulch. To propagate, divide established clumps in spring or autumn.

Stonecrop
Sedum telephium 'Purple Emperor'

Rich purple leaves and flowers for late-summer colour

Time to plant: spring or autumn

If it was twice the height, there would be no hesitation in describing *Sedum telephium* 'Purple Emperor' as tall, dark and handsome, but as it barely reaches waist level it will have to make do with being praised for its dusky good looks alone.

This purple-leaved perennial grows to 60cm (24in)-high and thrives in slightly alkaline, stony soil. It is best in full sun, which intensifies the decadent rich hues of the foliage. These fleshy, succulent leaves also give the plant excellent drought resistance.

Perfect at the front of a border, 'Purple Emperor' will make a large, bushy clump and boasts starry red flowers that are a magnet for bees and butterflies from late summer to mid-autumn. The faded flowerheads can be left in place to add structural interest at the start of winter.

TIPS

For bushier plants that flower slightly later, cut the top growth down by half at the end of May. Divide congested clumps in autumn. To make more plants, take softwood cuttings in early summer.

Lilac
Syringa pubescens subsp. *patula* 'Miss Kim'

Compact lilac with heavenly scented flowers – perfect for a small garden

Time to plant: all year round

Many lilacs are unruly, deciduous shrubs that demand a lot of space. Not 'Miss Kim' – she's well behaved and slow growing, with an upright habit. The plant eventually makes a 2m (6½ft)-high mound which retains its shape with the minimum of intervention from a pair of secateurs.

Of course, nobody grows lilac for its shape alone, and 'Miss Kim' is equally blessed with strongly scented flowers from late spring into early summer. These appear in great profusion at the end of the branches, the tightly packed clusters made up of masses of dark purple buds that open to reveal lavender-pink, tubular flowers. And as a final flourish, the green leaves turn purple in autumn, before falling.

Lilacs like a sunny spot and do best in alkaline soil, even quite thin chalky soil.

TIPS
To help establish a strong root system, always water regularly after planting. Maintain an attractive, rounded shape by removing any wayward branches. You can propagate by taking greenwood cuttings in summer.

Century plant
Agave americana 'Mediopicta'

Colourful succulent for year-round interest

Time to plant: spring – summer

Found in sun-drenched parts of Mexico, this imposing succulent is known as the century plant as it was once thought that the plant took a hundred years to produce its towering flower spike. In fact it only takes half this time, but if you still don't have the patience to wait, grow it for its architectural shape alone.

'Mediopicta' makes a large rosette of leathery leaves that curve gently outwards as they grow. A bright yellow stripe runs down the centre of each leaf, sandwiched between narrow bands of blue. The edges are armed with a row of dangerous red spines, and each leaf terminates in a viscous-looking needle.

Perfect for a sunny spot in a coastal garden or mild area, this agave is best planted on a slope so rainwater can run away from the roots. In colder areas, grow it in a pot and overwinter it in a frost-free place.

TIPS
Tidy up the plant by snipping off any dying leaves. If necessary, improve the drainage before planting by adding horticultural grit. Propagate by removing any rooted baby plants in spring.

Scots heather
Calluna vulgaris

Adds evergreen structure and summer colour

Time to plant: spring or autumn

A native of moorland, *Calluna vulgaris*, or Scots heather, is a tough little evergreen that will put up with the most punishing weather conditions. The plant found in the wild is too unruly to grow in gardens, but it has given rise to hundreds of well-behaved varieties that thrive in a sunny spot in acidic soil (if you don't have acidic soil, you can grow it in a pot filled with ericaceous compost).

Garden-worthy varieties reach 10–50cm (4-20in) tall and generally have green foliage and flowers that appear from July into autumn. Among the best choices are the white-flowering 'My Dream', pink 'Elsie Purnell', and 'Beoley Gold' whose white flowers contrast well against its yellow leaves.

TIPS
Water newly planted heathers regularly until established, and keep plants bushy by trimming in early spring. Propagate by taking cuttings in July.

Sedge
Carex

Flexible bronze leaves that look great moving in the wind

Time to plant: all year round

The tough, pliable foliage of the bronze-leaved varieties of carex allow them to thrive in exposed, windy sites and coastal locations where the attractive blades add movement to a garden as they flitter in the breeze. Carex are sedges, a handsome group of grass-like plants that make dense clumps; some have perky, upright foliage and others rise then arch like an ornamental fountain.

The bronze varieties of carex are the perfect foil for colourful perennials or as specimens in their own right. Growing to 20–60cm (8–24in) high, some of the best to look out for are *Carex buchananii*, *C.comans*, *C. comans* bronze-leaved, *C. flagellifera* and *C. testacea*.

Plant them in well-drained, moisture-retentive soil in either sun or dappled shade.

TIPS

Put on a pair of gloves and remove the dead foliage by carefully combing your fingers from the bottom to the top of the plant. You can make more plants by dividing the clumps in spring.

Mountain knapweed
Centaurea montana 'Alba'

A flurry of snowy-white flowers loved by bees and butterflies

Time to plant: spring or autumn

Look down on the intricate white flower of this perennial and you'll see it has more than just a passing resemblance to a delicate snowflake. These lovely flowers, which are about the size of a golf ball, burst from thistle-like buds in late spring and continue to appear in lesser numbers until autumn, their presence attracting bees and butterflies from far and wide.

Centaurea montana 'Alba' is a variety of mountain knapweed, which is native to many parts of Europe, where it grows on the lower slopes of mountains. In gardens it's ideal in a border or wildlife-friendly area and spreads quickly via a network of underground stems to make a dense mat of green-grey foliage, 45cm high by 60cm (18 x 24in) wide.

Fairly easy going, it's happy in free-draining, dry or moist soil, in either sun or part shade.

TIPS
Growth can become floppy, so stake the plants in spring. To make more plants, divide large clumps in autumn.

Sea holly
Eryngium bourgatii 'Picos Blue'

Electric-blue flowers on tough stems for weeks of colour and structure

Time to plant: spring – autumn

With a common name like sea holly, it should be no surprise that *Eryngium bourgatii* 'Picos Blue' does well in gardens lashed by coastal winds. But despite its reputation for being as tough as old boots, this herbaceous perennial is more than just utilitarian, thanks to its striking flowers.

Growing to just 40cm (16in)-high, this is one of the most compact sea hollies, forming a clump of spiny, silver-veined leaves that from mid-summer are hidden beneath many robust multi-branched stems. Rising like antlers, these are topped with electric-blue flowers.

Perfect in a coastal garden, 'Picos Blue' can also be grown in a border or gravel garden. It has a long tap-root and likes full sun and soil that drains readily.

TIPS

Leave the fading flowers as the seed heads will perk up the border in autumn – cut them to the ground in late winter. Divide large clumps in spring.

Veronica
Hebe 'Nicola's Blush'

Pink and white flowers from summer to winter

Time to plant: all year round

'Nicola's Blush' makes a bushy shrub that has amazing, long-lasting flowers. From early summer, spikes of pink appear which turn to white as they mature to give the plant an eye-catching, two-tone effect. This hebe really earns its keep as the flowers are produced for many months, sometimes well into the New Year, and it's a great choice for a wildlife garden as bees and butterflies just can't keep away.

A compact evergreen, this shrub only grows to 60cm (24in)-high. Its narrow green leaves have red margins – and in winter these turn an attractive shade of purple.

Incredibly easy to grow, 'Nicola's Blush' thrives in mild coastal areas, happily putting up with salt-laden winds. Plant it in a sunny spot in soil that is free draining and moisture retentive.

TIPS
Prune only to remove any branches that spoil its attractive shape. You can take cuttings in late summer and root in a propagator with bottom heat.

Hydrangea
Hydrangea macrophylla 'Rotschwanz'

Clouds of colourful summer flowers

Time to plant: all year round

Many hydrangeas grow into large, bloated shrubs, but this compact lacecap variety is perfect for smaller spaces and will thrive in exposed conditions in mild areas across the south and west of the UK.

At 1.2m (4ft) tall, 'Rotschwanz' may be vertically challenged in comparison to other hydrangeas that can reach 2m (6½ft), but it is perfectly formed, making a well-shaped bush and its green leaves take on a reddish tinge in autumn.

From July until autumn, this deciduous shrub is covered in clouds of flowers. On acidic soil the flattened heads have deep crimson, slightly puckered flowers arranged around the mass of smaller flowers in the centre. On alkaline soil the larger flowers are red.

Plant this hydrangea in moist but well-drained soil in dappled shade.

TIPS

Add a thick layer of mulch around plants in spring to help retain moisture in the soil. Remove old flowerheads in spring, cutting stems back to the nearest pair of healthy buds.

Sea lavender
Limonium sinuatum 'Petite Bouquet'

Easy-to-grow annual for vivid splashes of quick colour

Time to sow seeds: late winter – early spring

Some call this half-hardy annual statice, but its other name of sea lavender gives a big hint as to the kind of growing conditions it prefers. Found on coastal cliffs or mountain-sides in parts of the Mediterranean, this easy-to-grow flower may be small, but it's a tough cookie and will thrive in harsh conditions.

'Petite Bouquet' is a compact, bushy plant about 30cm (12in) tall, with stout spikes of papery flowers on stiff, bristly branches, appearing from mid-summer to September. Each packet of seeds will produce a mix of flower colours, from blue, white and pink to purple and yellow.

Extremely drought tolerant, this plant prefers to bask in the sun and likes soil that drains freely.

TIPS

Sow the seed indoors and then plant out in late spring or early summer.
Always ensure that the soil has adequate drainage – add horticultural grit if necessary. After flowering, consign the fading plants to the compost bin.

Variegated maiden grass
Miscanthus sinensis var. *condensatus* 'Cabaret'

A show-stopping grass for autumn interest

Time to plant: all year round

'Cabaret' is an apt name for this grass – growing up to 2.4m (8ft) tall, it makes a dramatic clump of ribbon-like leaves with dark green margins and snow-white stripes running from top to bottom down the centre. From autumn, the show is extended by a flurry of long-lasting copper-coloured plumes that rise high above the foliage and can be left to add interest over winter. With such impressive attributes, it demands to be grown centre stage as a specimen plant with a supporting cast of shorter grasses and perennials.

Despite its attractive looks, this miscanthus is unlikely to be damaged by wind due to its tough, flexible foliage. It likes to bask in the sun and is tolerant of many soils as long as they are well drained.

TIPS

Prune out any stems that revert to pure green. Cut down the foliage in spring to just above the emerging new shoots. You can make more plants by dividing the clump in spring.

Rosa mundi rose
Rosa gallica 'Versicolor'

Delicately scented, opulent pink flowers

Time to plant: spring or winter

If your hedge does a great job as a windbreak, but is in dire need of an injection of colour, try a shot of *Rosa gallica* 'Versicolor'. Commonly known as rosa mundi, this large shrub is ideal as part of a hedge and bears flamboyant, semi-double, ruffled blooms for several weeks in early summer.

Each bloom is slightly scented, with light pink petals that are liberally splashed with a darker shade of pink. At the centre is a glowing mass of sunny yellow stamens. If you don't deadhead the flowers, you'll get lots of marble-sized, bright red hips in autumn.

Grow this ancient rose (it's been around since the 16th century) in moist but free-draining soil, preferably in a sunny spot, where it will reach 82cm (32in) tall.

TIPS

Prune after flowering, reducing the sideshoots by about two-thirds and the upright shoots by about a third – leave some flowers for a good display of hips. In dry summers, water regularly.

Chilean potato tree
Solanum crispum

Fast-growing climber with scented flowers

Time to plant: spring or autumn

Need a plant to quickly cover a fence, wall or unsightly garden structure? Look no further than *Solanum crispum*. The Chilean potato tree, as it's commonly known, is a vigorous semi-evergreen climber which will quickly clamber to a height of 6m (20ft), providing its branches can be supported against a trellis or network of wires.

From summer until early autumn, the ends of the whippy shoots bear clusters of tiny, purple-blue, scented flowers with a contrasting yellow centre – the sharp-eyed will notice that these resemble potato flowers, a plant to which it's closely related.

Grow in fertile, well-drained soil and protect it over winter in exposed sites with a drape of horticultural fleece. The roots can be insulated by applying a thick layer of mulch in autumn.

TIPS
Prevent strong winds from damaging the whippy growth by regularly tying in any wayward stems to their supports. Prune the plant in early spring to keep it within its allotted space. You can propagate it by taking semi-ripe cuttings in summer.

Thyme
Thymus serpyllum 'Annie Hall'

Aromatic, ground-covering plant for gaps in paving

Time to plant: all year round

Native to such inhospitable places as barren moorland and rocky ground, *Thymus serpyllum* is a European native that spreads rapidly to make a dense mat of foliage which shrugs off gusty blasts easily.

'Annie Hall' has much lighter pink flowers than the creeping thyme found growing in the wild, but it has all of its tolerance of harsh weather. It's also incredibly hard wearing, and can be planted in gaps between paving slabs where its tiny green leaves will release their distinctive fragrance whenever trodden on.

This plant likes free-draining soil in sun and will spread to 45cm (18in) via a network of stems that root whenever they touch the ground. Masses of flowers crown the plant in summer, attracting bees and butterflies.

TIPS
To keep plants compact and within bounds, prune back after flowering. You can make more plants by lifting and dividing clumps in spring.

Laurustinus
Viburnum tinus 'Gwenllian'

Evergreen structure and stunning winter flowers

Time to plant: all year round

If you need a plant to chase away the winter blues, look no further than *Viburnum tinus* 'Gwenllian'. From late winter to early spring, this shrub is splashed with dense clusters of pink buds that open to reveal dazzling white flowers. These contrast brilliantly with the shiny, evergreen, dark leaves. Later in the year, this shrub carries masses of long-lasting, near-black berries.

'Gwenllian' reaches about 2.4m (8ft) tall and is a more compact form of the common laurustinus (*Viburnum tinus*). It can put up with a bit of a battering, as long as it's grown in fertile, free-draining soil. It tolerates air pollution and is happy in sun or part-shade in an exposed, north-facing position or a seaside garden that is lashed by wind.

TIPS
Minimal pruning is needed – simply cut it back to keep an attractive shape after flowering. You can take cuttings from semi-ripe wood in summer.

Index

Picture credits

BBC Books and *Gardeners' World Magazine* would like to thank the following for providing photographs. While every effort has been made to trace and acknowledge all photographers, we should like to apologize should there be any errors or omissions.

Torie Chugg p119, p139, p141, p183; Eric Crichton p59, p65, Sarah Cuttle p125, p131, p133; Paul Debois p47, p127, p157, p203; Peter Durkes p23; Jason Ingram p25, p33, p43, p55, p71, p75, p85, p93, p97, p103, p109, p111, p115, p121, p123, p135, p137, p145, p147, p149, p151, p155, p181, p187, p191, p193, p205, p211; Neil Holmes p35, p69, p129; Lynn Keddie p51, p117, p153; David Markson p95; Stephen Marwood p13; David Murray p39, p91, p159; Adam Pasco p15; Clay Perry p19; Tim Sandall p11, p17, p31, p41, p49, p53, p57, p61, p77, p79, p81, p87, p89, p99, p101, p107, p113, p143, p163, p173, p175, p177, p185, p189, p209; John Trenholm p73, p83, p105, p165, p171, p195, p207; William Shaw p161, p167, p179; Jo Whitworth p21, p45, p63, p67, p169, p213; Mark Winwood p37, p201; *Gardeners' World Magazine* p27, p29, p197, p199.